HOW TO VIDEO GAME ALL BY YOURSELF

10 steps, just you and a computer

by Matt Hackett

How to Make a Video Game All By Yourself

© 2024 Valadria
ISBN 978-1-7365762-0-5
All rights reserved

v1.2.0

TABLE OF CONTENTS

1. You Are a Producer
2. Scratch Your Itch
3. The Video Game Building Blocks
4. Pick a Game Engine
5. Make the Game You Want to Play
6. Find the Fun
7. Manage Your Scope
8. The Player Experience
9. Iterate to the Finish Line
10. Ship It!

About the Author

Hello. I'm **Matt Hackett**, also known as `richtaur` (/ˈrikˌtôr/). I've been playing video games my entire life. Somehow, to me, *making* them is even more fun and addictive than *playing* them. And even more challenging! I've poured a whole lotta love into this book, but if you need some convincing, here's a little bit about me:

I've been making games for 30 years and working in the games industry for over a decade. My indie games have sold over 50,000 copies and the games I created for big companies have been played by tens of millions of players. For over 6 years, my friend and collaborator Geoff Blair and I spent hundreds of hours having in-depth discussions about game production on our podcast, *Lostcast*. In addition to dozens of hobby creations, the games I've made "all by myself" include *Indie Game Sim*, a game about game development. How meta! Read more about me at `richtaur.com`

I love making video games. Let's get started on yours.

> I DON'T BELIEVE THAT THERE'S A RIGHT WAY TO MAKE GAMES.
>
> DEREK YU

You are the force that will drive this project to the finish line. Your steady hand steers the ship safely to shore. Without you, the ship will drift out to sea, unfinished.

When something needs to be done, you either find a way to outsource it or roll up your sleeves and do it yourself. You are the fuel that powers the engine of your video game. The time you spend on your project pushes it forward, ever closer to the finish line.

You are a video game producer, responsible for shipping your video game. Welcome! Settle in and get comfortable in your new producer role.

Take Off Your Hat

There's a commonly used concept of "wearing a hat" when you're doing a certain job. When programming a video game, you're wearing your "programmer hat" and writing some code. For game design, put on your "game designer hat" and design away.

You're making a video game all by yourself, so you'll need to wear many hats over time. The hats will come and go, but when you're not wearing any particular hat, only *you* remain: the producer of your video game.

If you have your heart set on eventually wearing certain hats, don't worry. You'll be able to "hire" yourself for those roles down the road. In fact, doing so can be an important part of having the drive to finish your video game (something we'll discuss more in *Chapter 2: Scratch Your Itch*).

PRODUCER

ARTIST

NO HAT

COMPOSER

PROGRAMMER

ANIMATOR

SOUND ENGINEER

LEVEL DESIGNER

All By Yourself (But Not Really)

People don't really work completely alone. Making a video game "all by yourself" implies that nobody else is helping, but let's take a moment to acknowledge and appreciate the assistance we all enjoy.

This book was written on a modern computer. With its advanced operating system, elegant design, and hardware materials sourced from all over the world, it is a staggering feat of engineering. Its capabilities enable my work and without it, I couldn't be productive.

I also could not recreate it on my own from scratch. It comes from the work of others and I depend upon it to do mine.

> IF I HAVE SEEN A LITTLE FURTHER IT IS BY STANDING ON THE SHOULDERS OF GIANTS.
>
> SIR ISAAC NEWTON

Software engineers benefit from the code written and lessons learned by their predecessors decades ago. The software they worked so hard on would do nothing without the hardware to run it. Hardware engineers use best practices and methods learned by others in their field years and years earlier. Through dedication and hard work, technology improves over time and pushes us all forward.

Some developers have a desire to make everything from scratch. The idea of using a pre-built tool can feel like "cheating" in the process. This is understandable — sometimes an external tool can seem like a **black box**, a mysterious and unknown quantity that feels uncomfortable to use.

"**Not invented here**" is a commonly used software term. It refers to the tendency for software developers to prefer creating their own tools over using external ones. It's a natural line of thought; people want to feel capable and in control. The thing is, some external software or assets *will* inevitably worm their way into your video game. So it's best to get used to the idea.

IF YOU WISH TO MAKE AN
APPLE PIE FROM SCRATCH,
YOU MUST FIRST INVENT
THE UNIVERSE.

CARL SAGAN

Early in my career, I used to frown upon drag-and-drop game engines that preferred graphical user interfaces over writing source code by hand. At the time, moving away from source code felt like giving up control. Later I learned a simple truth that is more important to me than control:

Players don't care what technology was used to make the games they play.

You might find the technology interesting, but that's because you're a game producer, not your average gamer. Gamers just want good games.

The best tools are whatever tools (built by you or found elsewhere) that enable you to quickly and effectively complete the vision of your game. Nothing else is terribly relevant.

In addition to the accumulated knowledge and efforts of our peers, many of us are also lucky enough to have family, friends, and perhaps an online community to aid us in small ways. Our networks, however humble, will lend us their time, advise us, play our game, and give us feedback and support.

You're producing a video game all by yourself ... but not really. Everybody who makes video games benefits from the aid of other people's hard work and support. Recognize and credit the help you receive.

Wield the Web

Thanks to the Internet, it's never been easier to make a video game. Those who know where to look will find open source libraries, free assets, public domain intellectual property, and completely finished tutorial games. The online game development world is full of fruit ripe for the plucking.

Although you're going solo, the invisible hand of the Internet will help guide you to the finish line. The free library you learned from or even incorporated directly into your game, the package of assets you bought, the sound effects you downloaded and tweaked, or the article you read that helped you understand the complicated process of signing applications for the Apple ecosystem — this is all out there and you should take advantage of it.

Making a video game all by yourself can be lonely and harrowing, but the Internet is here to help. How *much* help you accept is up to you.

You don't need to directly interact with other people but it can be wise to ethically leverage the work of others when possible. Some of you reading this will want to outsource almost all of the video game development process, while others will insist on lovingly crafting as much of your video game by yourself as you humanly can. It's a broad spectrum, a sliding scale with room for everyone.

There's no judgment here, only video game creation.

Given the daunting amount of information out there, your ability to quickly search for and correctly parse information online is a critical skill when it comes to shipping a video game by yourself. Search engines are your entry points into the world's accumulated knowledge. The better you are at using these tools, the more effective a producer you'll be.

Your goal is to become fluent in Internet searching. Specifically, you need to be able to craft custom search queries and parse the results for the answers you need.

Video game development search results will often direct you to forums or other online communities where people have collaborated together to solve their problems. The answer to *your* unique question will often be split between a dozen or more tabs in your web browser. This process of combination and elimination can be intimidating but is normal and necessary. Cross-referencing information that others have posted from completely different websites can often be exactly how to find the answer to your obscure game development issue.

While making a video game by yourself, you will encounter some very hairy problems along a wide array of categories. As the producer, these problems are in the way of shipping and therefore your sworn enemies. Learn to wield the web like a sword to defend yourself and push forward.

On Imposter Syndrome

Imposter syndrome is a psychological pattern in which a person doubts their abilities and feels like a fraud. This syndrome has an especially strong effect on people who make video games. The games industry is so vast, with so many different disciplines that it's easy to feel like an insignificant, unworthy grain of sand on an endless beach.

The line between an obscure video game and a huge "overnight" success can be razor-thin. The knowledge, skills, and experience needed to make a video game are significant. These factors empower imposter syndrome and make aspiring game developers feel like quitting before they even get started.

The good news is that almost everybody feels this way at some point in their journeys. Even the most prolific and successful game developers have had moments of panic, bouts of embarrassment, and feelings of fraudulence. You are not alone.

Imposter syndrome is a waste of time and energy. Keep this in mind:

You are a video game producer.

Anyone who rejects this is wrong. The proof that you are a video game producer is that you are currently producing a video game, full stop. Shut out anything that contradicts this.

I DON'T KNOW WHAT I'M DOING. EVERYTHING I'VE DONE IN MY LIFE I'VE JUST MADE UP AS I WENT ALONG. THAT'S WHAT EVERYONE IS DOING. THAT'S HOW LIFE WORKS.

TOMMY REFENES

Chapter 2: Scratch Your Itch

Video games are notoriously difficult to make. You've got a tough road ahead, littered with the failed attempts of many skilled creators. If you're going down this road, especially alone, you'd better make sure you're going in the direction you intended.

Now, you've probably heard amazing stories of individuals making a video game (largely) by themselves, sometimes including the fame and riches that followed. These stories are few and far between, and do not represent a typical game developer's experience. For every success story there are thousands more of those who failed, taking tolls on their personal lives.

Proceed with caution.

GAME DEVELOPMENT
IS THE DARK SOULS OF
SOFTWARE DEVELOPMENT.

YE OLDE GAME DEVELOPER SAYING

Here in this book, the desire to become rich or famous is not a valid itch. There are infinite ways to become either of those things, and making video games is one of the most technical, challenging, and time-consuming among them. You'll likely have better luck in other mediums.

There's probably a deeper reason you want to make a *video game* specifically. What is it? The desire to create your own version of a favorite game? A unique game idea you've always wanted to play, but nobody has made? A clever concept that you feel compelled to share with the world?

Dig deep. Where does it itch?

It might be that you don't know where your itch is yet, and that's okay. If you didn't have an itch at all, you probably wouldn't be reading this book. So you have an itch, you just need to locate it.

It could be that you're a generalist, happy to simply exist in the game development space, piecing things together in whichever way brings you happiness. If you keep your eyes open and go exploring, you may find a specific discipline that speaks to you.

Remember: yours alone is the hand that guides your project to the finish line. Since it's all up to you, you need to be aware of what burning imperative gives you fuel.

Find your fire.

Where Does It Itch?

Some of you reading this know the exact location of your itch. It's *right there* and it's been driving you crazy. It's laser-focused, singular in nature. There's this *one part* of game development that's pushing you forward and launching you out of bed in the morning.

For those lucky few, it's time to scratch your itch like mad. Prepare to hire yourself for your itchiest job. Your project's success is likely tied to the scratching of this particular itch, so lean into it and accept it fully.

For the rest of us, we might have some searching to do. "Doctor help, it itches," we say, while perusing game development forums and admiring screenshots. There's an itch here, for sure. Game development is seductive, alluring ... and those of us that "have the bug" are often up late, tuned in to the siren's call.

If you can't find your itch, it's time to go exploring.

Explore

As we discussed, some of you reading this know exactly why you're here. Your muse speaks loud and true, directly in your ear. You might not *need* this section, but it wouldn't hurt you to explore either. You could find something that surprises you.

If you're not sure where your itch is, it's time to visit the buffet and sample various dishes. Try developing a very simple app, drawing a few sprites, creating some sound effects, or writing a game design document. Find your favorite game developers' websites, look at their job descriptions, and see what sounds fun to you. Watch some behind-the-scenes videos. Listen to some podcasts. Dig around.

Immerse yourself and have fun.

Maybe nothing clicks right away, or maybe all of game development is appealing, and you are ravenous, eager to gobble it all up yourself. That's completely fine.

Down the road, don't be afraid to think again. You might find that, oh, you don't really enjoy drawing dozens of sprites by hand the way you thought you would. Or nope, it's not fun for you to design hundreds of levels by yourself like you thought it might be. The more you know about yourself the better you can decide which tasks you'll do yourself, and which you'll outsource (or automate).

Wander around and explore. Get a little lost, learn a lot.

Learn To Say No

I'm going to be straight with you. If you don't learn to say "no" you will never finish your video game.

FOCUS IS ABOUT SAYING NO.

STEVE JOBS

Yes, you *can* craft every single aspect of your game by hand. You can choose every pixel, write every line of code, compose every note of music, and create every sound effect from scratch. It can be done, and sure, it would be very impressive.

But we all live finite, mortal lives, and at some point you have to let certain things go. The good news is that when you do let go, you're free to spend more time focusing on the itches you're most eager to scratch.

It's okay to try on a hat but eventually end up outsourcing that hat. I'm primarily a game programmer, designer, and artist, but I also really love making music. If you dig a little bit online, you'll stumble upon some video game remixes I made from classic games like *Kung Fu* and *Ironsword: Wizards & Warriors II*.

But I had to give up making music (at least, for a while). For me, I realized that creating music felt like slow, hard work. I find it fun but it can be laborious. I can fly when programming or drawing sprites, but when making music my maximum speed was a slow crawl at best.

I also am lucky to have a prolific composer friend named Joshua Morse who can really crank out fantastic video game music. Joshua quickly made great music for many of my games, informing my decision to put music creation down so I could focus on other tasks.

You can't say "yes" to everything. At some point you've got to narrow your focus, and that means saying "no" and meaning it.

Find Your Happy Place

Your **happy place** is somewhere you can truly say you're content. Now is the time to be selfish, now is the time to be creative, now is the time to dig deep and be honest about what really, truly means something to you. Don't just *find* what scratches your itch, manifest it into reality and begin to surround yourself with it.

If it's football players riding dinosaurs, you need to go with that. If it's designing the subtle variations between different striations of rock formations, yes go with it. Now's the rare time when you can be weird and specific. You're making an independent game by yourself, and indie games by nature can be experimental and unexpected. *This* particular game should be tailored to your unique tastes, whatever they may be.

If your project isn't truly, deeply making you fall in love with it then you'll have a harder time finishing it. When you work on it, it needs to feel good, like home.

Bring It Home

Find your itch (or at least *an* itch) and move towards scratching it. If later you discover that you were wrong about your itch, or find something else that's itchier, that's fine. Come back to this chapter and repeat the process. Consider this a loop you can revisit anytime with no remorse.

Don't feel bad if you get lost or went down the wrong path for a while. Some artists spend their entire lifetimes chasing their itches. Itches change and you'll be learning a lot while exploring. Just remember to always move forward, make decisions, and occasionally ship things. Don't be constantly on the chase.

Make a short list of the kinds of games that are small enough for you to realistically finish but also satisfy your itch. Finding your itch is one thing, but we are making a video game here. It's time to bring the puzzle pieces together and imagine a finished video game.

Chapter 3: The Video Game Building Blocks

Video games are complicated machines, composed of many moving parts that need to harmonize together. When making a video game all by yourself, it's especially important to understand the fundamental building blocks you'll be using. After all, you are the producer and the buck stops with you.

This is a relatively dry chapter, so I hope your itch is strong enough to keep you excited through the fundamentals. You need to know this stuff.

So, what makes a video game?

To exist, a video game needs: presentation, input, and feedback.

Let's dive in.

THE VIDEO GAME BUILDING BLOCKS

Presentation (Graphics)

A video game must have some way to communicate to the player. Although a game could communicate via audio or other means alone, the vast majority of video games display visual graphics via one or more flat, two-dimensional (2D) screens.

Back in the 1960s, games featured big fat black and white pixels like those in the original *Pong*. As technology improved, the amount of colors increased and the pixel size decreased. Today we have immersive, realistic three-dimensional (3D) simulations that can look almost exactly like the real world.

The visual presentation of your video game is very likely tied to your itch. You might already have a pretty good idea of what you want your game to look like, but don't be afraid to get creative and think outside the pixel (especially while exploring). Old and underused rendering techniques can both make a game easier to develop and help it stand out visually among its peers.

There's an interesting game called *Stone Story RPG* that displays only pure, simple, black-and-white ASCII-art. Certainly this unique style came with its own challenges to implement, but the developer found a creative way to dodge the very expensive task of creating realistic, high fidelity artwork.

The aesthetic certainly isn't for everyone, and while some might say the visual style is a turnoff, I'd argue that it's so interesting it gets mentioned in books.

Keep in mind that simple aesthetics can help you finish your game faster and smarter.

2D VS 3D

In video games, 2D and 3D are completely different, yet exactly the same.

Without getting deep into AR & VR (augmented reality & virtual reality), video games are largely rendered to flat 2D surfaces. Computer monitors, television sets, and mobile devices are the most common rendering targets. Under the hood the game might be using 2D or 3D technology (or a combination of both), but the output is the same: a rectangle of pixels.

THE 2D YOU SEE

COULD BE 3D

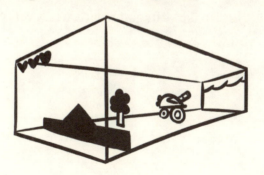

Dimensions often become intermingled in video games. An entirely 3D game like a first-person shooter might have a 2D user interface. Some games that are rendered in 2D might use a 3D physics engine to control their logic.

There's even a term, **2.5D**, for games that live somewhere in the middle. For example: a side-scrolling platformer game might constrain all of its action to two dimensions, but use 3D technology to render its graphics.

The software needed to create 2D versus 3D assets are very different, but many of the skills are compatible. The takeaway is to not get lost between the dimensions, because they can be interchangeable. Just make your game with whatever technology makes sense to you.

Input

In a video game, players must be able to participate or it's not really a game. The input from the player can be minimal — pressing a gigantic "Win" button or beginning a simulation with configurable settings can certainly be considered player input.

The most common forms of input include keyboards, mice, gamepads, and touchscreens. Some video games get very creative with input, such as *The Legend of Zelda: Phantom Hourglass* which (spoiler) requires players to blow into microphones to extinguish in-game fires. Another example is the *Playdate* handheld gaming device which lets players use a weird crank attached to the side of the device to control its games.

Input might seem like a trivial part of making your video game, but the decisions you make about input can have big impacts on your project. The bottom line is: if you make a video game that can get by with only one form of input, you are making life easier on yourself. Games like *Chess* are simple enough that they can be played with only a mouse (or touch device). There's nothing about it that makes players insist on a keyboard or beg for a gamepad.

You may want to avoid certain forms of input because they are inherently **hungry**. When a feature is hungry, it practically demands additional work and isn't simple to finish. Adding keyboard support is one thing, but keyboard support is best when highly configurable. Not all players want their movement tied to the WASD keys or use keyboards in your native language.

Gamepads can be especially hungry. Gamepads can position their buttons in different places, report their data in unexpected formats, or send noisy data to your game. These issues may result in an unplayable video game for players with certain gamepads.

That said, I am madly in love with gamepads. I love collecting them, looking at them, and especially using them to play video games. I have made a few touch-only video games in my day, only to eventually realize that *my* happy place is happiest with gamepads. I added gamepad support to one of my projects and immediately fell more in love with it. Gamepad support added fuel to my fire and gave new life to the project.

Supporting keyboards and gamepads warrants settings, menus, configuration ... By adding gamepad support I designed myself into that corner, but at least I was aware of it and able to plan ahead for that extra work. My hands are itchy for gamepads and when I can put one in my own hands through my own games, my itch is better scratched. But that's me. You've got your own itches to scratch.

Be careful what you're signing up for and thoughtfully decide which forms of input to support. If your itch includes some form of input, be sure to include it. Otherwise, keep it simple.

Feedback & The Game Loop

After a player has given a video game input, it's important for them to understand the result of that input, or it isn't much of a game. "Did you win? Did you lose? What happened?"

When you play a game of *Rock, Paper, Scissors* with a friend, your input is the option you choose. The critical feedback you receive is the option your friend chooses. Once you see that you chose *rock* and they chose *paper*, you can determine that the game is over and they won. Without that feedback, you'd never know who won the game.

Most video games do not immediately end after receiving input. Instead, they implement a **game loop**.

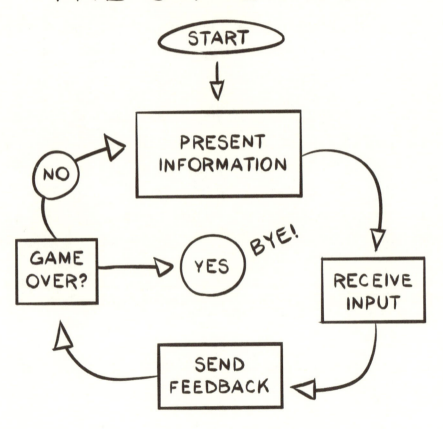

Once a video game starts, it begins its game loop:

1. **Present** information to the player.
2. Receive **input** from the player.
3. Provide **feedback** regarding the player's input.
4. Check for a **Game Over** condition.
5. If the game didn't end, **return to step 1** and repeat.

The recurring loop creates room for gameplay, where the player can experiment with mechanics and demonstrate their skill by overcoming challenges. While looping, the game updates its state based on player input.

A **turn-based** game is one that waits for user input before continuing its game loop. A game is called **real time** when its loop is continuous, running regardless of whether the player is providing input or not.

Video games usually have some kind of Game Over condition that ends the game. For example, when a player's character falls into lava, they are killed and the Game Over condition is triggered. If a player passes the final challenge, the game ends with the player victorious. Roll the credits!

Player input and the game loop are fundamental components of the video game building blocks and important to understand. Along with presentation and feedback, they make up the core fundamentals of a video game.

Phew! Now that we're past the dry part, are you ready for a **boss encounter**?

BEWARE!

HERE BE DRAGONS

Danger approaching! The next step you must take has defeated many brave warriors before you. Prepare for battle.

Not everyone who begins this book will finish it. Beyond that, only the very dedicated will actually execute the steps within. Making video games is hard, *especially* by yourself. My best guess is that most creators who don't finish this book will stop here, and perish climbing this mountain. Right here, right now.

Too scared or are you ready to press forward? Those that successfully emerge from the other end will be richly rewarded with the amazing skills to make video games.

YOU'RE FILLED WITH
DETERMINATION.

TOBY FOX

Chapter 4: Pick a Game Engine

As a producer, it's not absolutely necessary for you to learn how to program a video game yourself. Technically you could outsource this process by hiring a software developer to create the game for you. If that's what you have your heart set on, go for it. Much of the information in this book should still be helpful.

However, going down that path means making a lot of sacrifices and, in many ways, distancing yourself from the fate of your game. Someone else is doing the heavy lifting at that point, and it isn't really in the "all by yourself" spirit. At their core, video games are just software, so let's develop that software ourselves.

The good news is: **you got this**. Modern game engines are so full-featured and impressive that you don't even need to learn how to write source code to develop video games anymore! The perfect game engine for you is out there, we just gotta find it.

Know What to Look For

The goal of this chapter is for you to find and become relatively fluent in a **game engine**. The definition of "game engine" is pretty loose across the games industry, but let's define it as: software you can use to create complete, playable, distributable video games.

You don't need to actually produce a finished video game to verify that you've completed this step, but you do need to kick the tires and take your game engine for a ride. Buckle up.

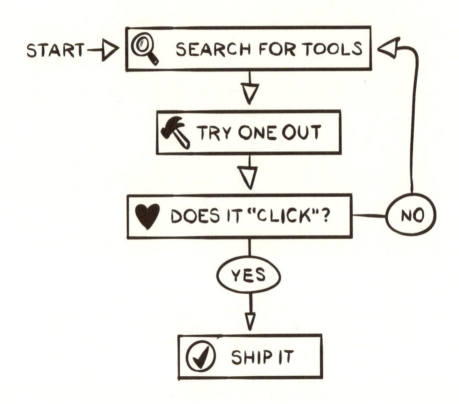

Some of you already have your game engine of choice and are committed to it: maybe you've been an avid *GameMaker* user for years, or perhaps you absolutely insist on using handwritten *C++* because that's what you became comfortable with in school. Maybe all this technology talk puts you to sleep because you just like to crank out simple narrative games in *Twine*. It's all good.

For the rest of you, it's time to find a game engine that you can work with. The options these days are overwhelming, but here are the traits to look for in your game engine:

1. Is capable of creating complete video games.
2. Scratches your itch.
3. "Clicks" with you.
4. Propels your game forward.

For #1, refer to *Chapter 3: The Video Game Building Blocks*. If a game engine that you find is capable of implementing all of the building blocks, then this requirement is satisfied.

It's also important for the game engine you choose to scratch your itch. Perhaps you prefer to be writing code in the *Python* language or maybe you don't want to be writing any code at all. Your game engine needs to scratch these itches or you'll remain itchy.

The game engine needs to **click** with you, meaning it simply makes sense and gives you good feelings. Complicated software like game engines have strong personalities of their own. Some will appeal to you while others will feel *off* somehow.

For a game engine to click you may need to spend a good chunk of time with it. You're looking for that moment when it all comes together, when you start to understand how to execute tasks without needing guides. Try browsing the documentation or watching tutorials to see if it's speaking your language.

Lastly, the game engine needs to be capable of *propelling your game forward*. Video game engines can be *especially* deep oceans and highly distracting. Make sure when you're using the game engine you're using it to make a video game, and not just lost in the weeds.

Cast a Wide Net

Begin by looking far and wide. Start by using your Internet search skills: search the web for "list of game engines". Current industry leaders include *Unity*, *GameMaker*, *Unreal Engine*, *Godot*, *Phaser* ... but this list will change dramatically over time.

Since you *Know What to Look For* from the previous section, you can eliminate many options that don't meet your requirements. For the rest, compile a list and start to kick the tires. Download the software, open it up, look around, and experiment.

Hello World

A **hello world** program is one that simply displays a greeting and exits. It's a classic programming pattern taught to students around the world and for good reason. By printing "Hello World" to your screen, you're showing evidence that the program executes without error. It demonstrates the ability to clearly communicate messages to the user.

Merely printing text is a good start, but not really enough for a video game. Your video game's equivalent of "Hello World" is a bit more complicated.

Refer again to *Chapter 3: The Video Game Building Blocks*. The "Hello World" of your video game should satisfy all of the basic building blocks required to ship a game. This includes:

1. Display graphics (some text, a 2D sprite, and/or a primitive 3D shape).
2. Detect input.
3. Output feedback.

In addition to displaying graphics, you'll likely also want to play a single sound effect and perhaps some music. Whatever is necessary to complete the bare-bones vision of your video game should be included here. Nothing fancy is needed yet, just the "Hello World" equivalent of these pieces. Barely enough to prove that it's all working fine is all you need right now.

When detecting input, the devices used to make your video game are the easiest places to start: your keyboard and mouse. You should also be able to detect whatever inputs your game will require (for example, input from a gamepad if that's important to you). For now, simply detecting that the input device exists and can be read is enough.

For the feedback portion, simply communicate to the user that their input was received. You could show some text, change a sprite, play a sound, or rotate a 3D cube — whatever shows the player that the game recognizes their input.

It's natural to stumble on even these basic steps. The engines you'll be researching are vastly complicated, capable of creating entire digital worlds. This causes the documentation and examples to be dense and intimidating. It can be frustrating to struggle so much on what feel like trivial tasks. We've all been there and it's okay.

At this stage in your journey it's more important to get the tasks done than to worry about speed and efficiency.

Learning these first baby steps can be especially painful, but you've gotta push forward. Luckily for us, online videos, tutorials, and forums are so rich and saturated now that they'll be able to answer any question you need to ask. Decide what your task is, *Wield the Web* to learn how to complete it, then get it done.

Once you've implemented the basics of your video game's "Hello World", ask yourself what you think of the game engine so far. Does it feel pretty good, maybe even intuitive, like it's helping you instead of indifferent to you? If not, move on. Maybe you'll revisit.

Be patient with this step! "Give me software I enjoy using that can make any video game I can imagine" is a big ask. Fortunately there are more options and competition out there than ever. The right fit for you exists, you just need to find it.

When in doubt: use whatever's most popular. Trust others to figure out which game engines are worth your time. The most popular platforms also tend to have the best documentation and communities available to help.

Time to Jam

Pick a game engine and let's jam! A **game jam** is a common term in the game development world: it's a short hackathon for game developers. In a game jam, developers crunch on very small projects in a short amount of time. A popular jam is *Global Game Jam* which lasts 3 days, but many jams last just one day or a whole week.

You can officially enter one of these jams if you'd like, or perform a self-imposed jam to reduce the pressure. Give yourself a hard limit of 24 hours, or spread out over a weekend, or even just one tight evening: whatever amount of time you can afford.

Many of these jams provide a **theme** for the developers to follow. Themes are often single-word concepts like "mercy" or "avoidance" that developers are meant to interpret and integrate into their games. You could give yourself a random theme to attempt but I think a good place to start is by doing a **master study** of one of your favorite simple games.

In a master study, the student attempts to reproduce the work of the master. When painting in art school, an artist might be assigned a study of *Mona Lisa* by Leonardo da Vinci. Obviously the student isn't expected to complete the entire painting and the quality of the work will by definition be lower than that of the master's. The point is to attempt, to stretch, to improve your skills.

The goal of the game jam is to learn and have fun. Ideally there's something playable at the end, but that's not necessary to get value out of the jam. I won't tell you how to jam, but I'd recommend grabbing your favorite game and trying to reproduce a small slice of it. Love the way Samus jumps in the *Metroid* games? Try to reproduce that jump and nothing else: cut the enemies, cut the environment, cut the forward movement if you need to. Just pick a small slice and try to build it.

Whatever you produce in the end, be happy with it. Even if it's incomplete ... *you* made it! Developing even simple portions of video games takes intelligence and dedication. Be kind and patient with yourself.

MASTER   STUDY

How to Get Unstuck

Remember that this chapter is brutal, slaying many brave warriors. So how are you dealing with the dragons? Some of you, dear readers, have surely gotten stuck in the devious depths of game development software. Don't be discouraged; it's a sticky web that ensnares many. Let's talk about how to get unstuck.

For starters, **keep a list** (or a spreadsheet) of the game engines you've tried, what they could/couldn't do, and what you did/didn't like about them. Eventually you can use this information to help you see the strengths and weaknesses of each engine and focus on exactly what you're looking for.

Move up the ladder. Video games are technically complex and it's easy to get lost in the making of them. One way to get unstuck is to move up the ladder, away from lower-level development like graphics and engines, and into higher-level development like mods and level editors.

Try plug-and-play packages. Online you can find 100% complete game engines ready for you to plug into and use to create your game. The *Unity Asset Store* and other online marketplaces offer plug-and-play packages like this, and there are even some free open source options available. There is a trade-off: you'll be at the mercy of the package's capabilities and when (or if) its developer updates it. You'll also need to learn how to use their specific package, which will likely be a large endeavor. But a package like this could propel your project forward.

Settling on a game engine can feel like a big commitment. Just remember that sticking to something and pushing forward is better than forever wandering.

Find Your Engine For Anything

Lastly, some of you reading this book are very interested in creating the assets for your game yourself. Whether it's music, 2D sprites, sound effects, or 3D models, you can make anything you need all by yourself. To find software to help you make your game's assets, you can use the steps in this chapter by replacing "game engine" in your searches with whatever you'd like to find.

For example, if you'd like to explore making music for your game, search for "music making software" or "list of music software". Most of the software you find in this manner are perfectly valid choices.

Try out the software, make a little something using it, and see how it makes you feel. Find documentation and tutorials to help you along. Similar to the game engine search, sometimes it will click with you and sometimes it won't. Keep track of what works and what doesn't, and with time you'll have software that enables you to make anything you can imagine.

Chapter 5: Make the Game You Want to Play

Now that you're ready to make a game, it's time to start thinking about what game you're going to make. This can be a daunting task, stumping even longtime games industry veterans. In his article *Finishing a Game*, game designer and *Spelunky* creator Derek Yu has some fantastic suggestions:

1. Games I want to make.
2. Games I want to have made.
3. Games I'm good at making.

These are excellent points and will help you determine what kind of game you should be making. Another condition I like to consider is: Games I want to play.

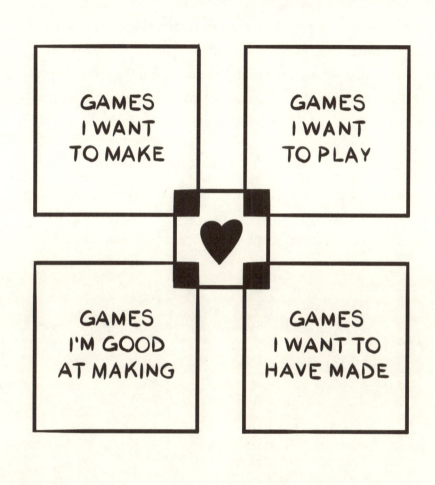

It might be that you have an itch to make a game that you don't necessarily *want* to play. Certainly some amazing games have been made by developers who were indifferent to (or even loathed) the type of game they were making. I'm not saying those developers shouldn't have made those games, of course, but happening to love playing the game you're making creates a more enjoyable developer environment for you.

Simply put: wanting to play the game you're working on reduces the friction of working on it.

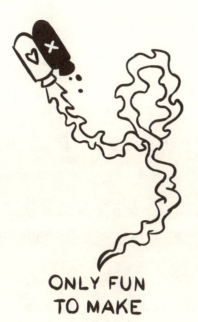

ONLY FUN
TO MAKE

FUN TO MAKE
<u>AND PLAY</u>

Making a Game is Playing That Game

When you're making a video game all by yourself, you're going to be the only person playing that game for most of its development. Testing any new content or feature is the same thing as playing that game.

Making a puzzle game? You'll need to attempt those puzzles over and over again while designing them.

Adding a jump mechanic? You'll need to repeatedly play with the jump to get it feeling good.

Adding a complicated quest? You'll need to repeatedly play through the steps of the quest to test them during development.

Since you must perform these tasks hundreds or thousands of times during development, it's preferable that you enjoy them. You'll be a happier developer and more likely to finish your project.

WRITING A BOOK IS READING THAT BOOK.
FILMING A MOVIE IS WATCHING THAT MOVIE.
MAKING A GAME IS PLAYING THAT GAME.

ME, I SAID THAT

Make it For You

You'll be playing your game a lot as you make it. You'll know every nook and cranny, so you should make yourself comfortable. Remember that this game is for you. You're the producer, the one at the center, ensuring everything gets done. Since you're doing it alone, you are the sole client, yours the only taste to appease. Since this is for *you*, have fun with it in *your* way.

Maybe part of your itch is to get your game into the hands of thousands of players all across the globe (and maybe after a lotta hard work you can get there), but in the meantime you are the first player. You're the only player that matters in the beginning, so it makes sense to double down on yourself and what you want.

Make your game opinionated and let yourself really come out. Speak loudly and pick a clear lane. The game should scream *you*. It's your home, your happy place. If you nurture your game in this way, you can create a delicious creative cycle.

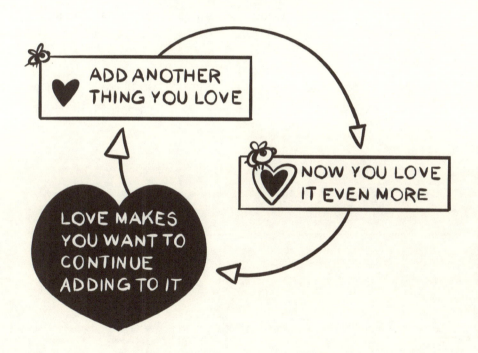

Does something you want to express feel too emotional, too political, too scandalous? This is not the time to care about that. Your game is not a stuffy corporate project that needs to appeal to the masses to please shareholders.

Your game is yours, yours alone, and can be as weirdly, uniquely you as you desire.

The more personal and *for you* it is, the more you'll love it, and the more likely that you'll be able to summon the strength to finish it.

Make it for you.

MOST GAMES

BORING SWORD

YOUR GAME

SHARK SWORD!

Prototype Until Happy

A **prototype** is a minimal, playable demonstration of a game concept. It doesn't need to look good or sound good but it should start to *feel* good. Prototyping is the best place to start with any new idea you're trying out.

It's okay to experiment with various prototypes before landing on one that you think you can take to the finish line. Video games are vast in their diversity. Finally zeroing in on the *one* type of game to make among dozens of cool ideas can be daunting.

Spend as much time in the exploratory phase as you need; it'll pay off later. Explore again, get lost on tangents, make a weekend game jam that you end up not wanting to continue on. It's all fine.

Game developers with freedom to explore sometimes climb to the top of a mountain, only to realize that they've climbed the wrong mountain. This is normal and okay.

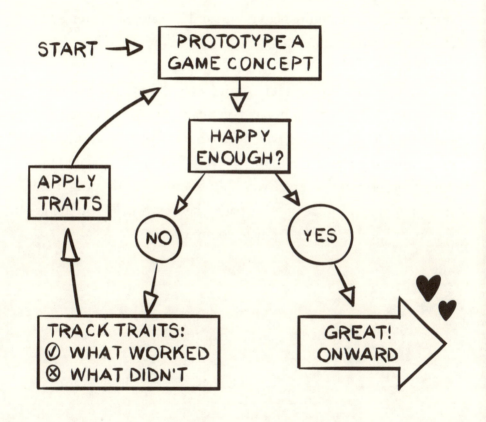

It can be frustrating to realize you've spent time and energy in the wrong direction. But the climbing strengthens you. You learned so much during your climb, and your muscles remember. Whether you can tell or not, you're better now, and you are more prepared for the next mountain.

As you iterate, it's important to record what did and did not work about each project. If you iterated on a game idea but it ended up not feeling "right" for you, why not? What did you like about the project that drew you to it in the first place? What did you end up not liking about it that made you want to move on? Keeping these traits in mind will guide you to a path where eventually you'll find the "right" project and be ready to commit further.

Remember: you are producing a video game. The goal is not to iterate forever. Iterate until you've got a game that you enjoy working on and playing. You enjoy it so much that you could imagine spending lots of time with it ... because you will need to in order to ship it.

Explore and iterate until you feel satisfied with your direction, then push on to the next step.

Chapter 6: Find the Fun

It's so easy for the hours to melt away when you're working on a video game. But are you having more fun working on the thing than playing the thing? Some of us find video games very fun to *make*, but the most important thing is making a game that's fun to *play*.

Make a Toy

Fun activities in video games often revolve around mechanics that can be thought of as toys.

Consider a standard, spherical ball used for sports and games. People all around the world love the dynamic between gravity and ball so much that they could play with it all day, entranced, constantly enjoying and learning. Even by themselves, all alone, the play of gravity has the potential to be infinitely entertaining and deep.

Similarly, in a platformer video game the joy of jumping can be instantly gratifying and delightful. In a puzzle game, it might be satisfying to simply scoot rocks around. Thinking of the core mechanic as an enjoyable toy can help you find the fun in your game.

Once the toy is established, game rules can be applied. Take for example a player enjoying a ball by themselves, kicking it against a wall for practice and exercise. Give them a goal and suddenly there's a game. Here's a brainstorm of ideas for rules:

1. Kick the ball against a tree 10 times in a row without missing.
2. Bounce the ball off your knees 30 consecutive times without dropping it.
3. Balance the ball on your head (no hands!) for 60 seconds.

Just as the play of ball and gravity is infinitely deep, the game rules can have infinite variety.

A game of *Association Football (Soccer)* includes 2 teams of 11 players running across a large field, restricted to their lower body to maneuver the ball into the opposing team's goal, all while abiding by civil rules to ensure safe and fair play. The outcome of any game must take into consideration the physique, speed, stamina, experience, skill, physical health, and mental state of all 22 players. The game is so infinitely complex, yet understandable, that it's easy to see why it's the most popular sport in the world.

One can also imagine the game with only 4 players. Or 100 players. Or what if the players were allowed to pick up and throw the ball? What if players had to hold their breath while they had the ball? No matter the rules, the underlying structure and physics of the game remain the same.

Game rules come and go and are easy to tweak later. Even after you've decided on a set of rules, you may still decide to add a different **game mode** that changes the rules of the game. Common game modes include "story", "survival", and "permadeath", each drastically changing the game rules. For now it's more important to find a fun toy to play with.

Get Lost

Your game should be very appealing to you at this point. In theory it's scratching your itch and it's the game you want to play. If it's not at least occasionally pulling you in, there could be a problem. If you can't get lost in your game, even just a little, then you haven't found the fun.

Once upon a time I was developing a real time action game. During development I had to test the flow of the game, going from beginning to end. To ensure a new feature worked correctly I just needed to start up a game, play through quickly, then check to see if the credits rolled as expected. I was on a simple mission.

While playing, however, the game pulled me into a trap! I came upon something irresistible — a rare drop of my favorite weapon — and it led to my death. I was having fun, immersed in the experience, and more eager to play than to make. This is what you want: to get lost in the fun of your game.

Time Yourself

How long a game takes to play is a common metric in the games industry. How long does one game session last? How long would it take a player to play through the game once, to "beat" the game? How long would it take a player to see every single piece of content in the game?

These are common questions gamers want to know in the real world, but for your purposes there are more relevant questions during development, including but not limited to:

1. How long can you currently play your game before losing interest?
2. How long does it take for you to speed run through your game as fast as you can?
3. How long would it take a brand new player to play through without having any prior knowledge about the game?

Having a basic idea of these metrics can help educate you about your work. It can be encouraging to learn that you've made several minutes of unique gameplay and you get the satisfaction of seeing this number increase over time.

Actually adding a timer to your game should be trivial. Simply render some text to the screen, maybe in a corner, that shows the elapsed time.

The Eureka Moment

At some point along the long road of development, something will open your eyes, surprise you, and delight you. That's your **eureka moment**.

In my real time action prototype, I was experimenting with some simple systems with basic rules, including:

1. When an item is destroyed, it can spawn another item.
2. When an enemy touches an item, the enemy picks it up.
3. Enemies with items can use them to attack the player.

One time two unarmed enemies were running at me. I threw a pitchfork at the first enemy, killing it, and destroying the pitchfork (causing the pitchfork to spawn a stick). The second enemy kept running at me, and happened to walk over the stick, which it picked up. Now having a weapon, the enemy threw it at me, killing me instantly and startling me.

I hadn't necessarily planned this sequence of events, they just happened because the systems and rules harmonized. That was the project's eureka moment and it proved to me that it had promise.

Be sure that the eureka moment comes from gameplay and not development. Video game development can at times be nebulous, confusing, and unpredictable. At some point, your game might have a bug that causes something to explode when it's not supposed to, surprising and delighting you. Or a sprite might suddenly render in the wrong place, making you laugh.

But those are *your* experiences making the game, not the experience *players* will have while playing it. Once you've found the fun, ensure the player is the one who gets to have it.

Presentation Matters

Sometimes the fun is there, it's just obscured under an unattractive layer of grime. It's fine to prototype video games quickly, being messy and throwing in placeholder graphics (or none at all). To find the fun, the mechanics are more important than the presentation ... but only to a point.

If a slice of cake tastes delicious but looks disgusting, nobody will want to eat it. Likewise if a game looks foul or sounds irritating, it's harder to find the fun. In this regard, a little bit of polish goes a long way.

MAKE IT PRESENTABLE

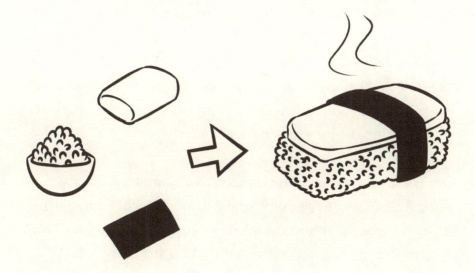

At this stage you don't have to implement production-ready presentation quality. But after you've found a fun toy, it can be beneficial to polish it up a bit and make it presentable. You can do this yourself if you're skilled at such things, or you can leverage the web to help you out.

Online you can find treasure troves of usable assets. Sprites, 3D models, animations, and more are free to use for those who know where to find them. Use your *Wield the Web* skills from *Chapter 1: You Are a Producer*. Common searches include "free 2D sprites" or "free to use 3D models". Be sure to check the details of the **license** attached to the assets. A license is a permit of authority that grants permissions to use the assets in certain ways.

One common type of license is a **Creative Commons license**. These licenses are just one of several public copyright licenses that enable the free distribution of otherwise copyrighted works. Sometimes these licenses are free to use, no strings attached. Sometimes they require attribution, or a link to the author's portfolio. Read the details to ensure you adhere to the license.

PLEASE THE SENSES

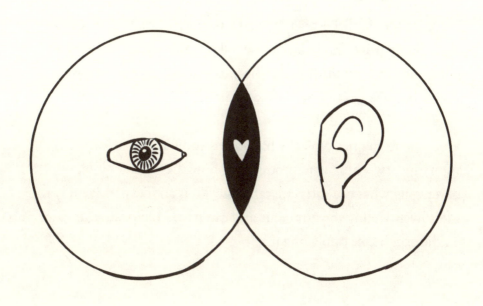

You could create your own assets or commission new ones directly from an artist, but I would caution against spending too much time or resources on assets at this stage of development. For now, you want to get something in place that's serviceable, and worry about final assets later when the project is further along.

Probably the single best way to make your game more presentable is by adding **juice**. In their seminal talk *Juice It or Lose It*, Martin Jonasson and Petri Purho describe juice as, "things that wobble, squirt, bounce around or make cute noises."

Video game engines typically have many tools available for scaling, animating, tweening, and modulating how the graphics look. Leveraging what the software can easily do is an inexpensive way to add a lively feeling to your game and can have a big positive impact on the experience of playing it.

IN VIDEO GAMES, JUICY THINGS ARE THINGS THAT WOBBLE, SQUIRT, BOUNCE AROUND OR MAKE CUTE NOISES.

MARTIN JONASSON, PETRI PURHO

Next think about audio. Get some sound effects: create them, purchase them, or find some with a Creative Commons or similar license that allows you to use them. Dig through the files listening for short, satisfying sounds. Even if you don't think you currently have a use for that sound, save it for later. If it's a pleasant sound effect that you can listen to over and over again, keep it and put it in your game somewhere. It'll improve the presentation and satisfy more senses.

Music has the same effect, but only add it if you need it and are ready for it. I find music to be a hungry feature that demands more attention. Players will want the ability to mute the music, which you should absolutely give them. (You will definitely want the ability to mute the music while developing the game.) Players will want the ability to lower or raise the volume, which you should probably give them, since that's a reasonable request.

Music can add lots of atmosphere and make the experience more polished, but it isn't always as easy to drop in as sound effects.

By now you should be a happy producer who is scratching your itch by making a fun game you want to play using your shiny new game engine. Things are looking good ...

Which means it's time for another **boss encounter**!

Prepare yourself.

Chapter 7: Manage Your Scope

The previous boss encounter in *Chapter 4: Pick a Game Engine* has left many of your peers defeated. They never found game engines that "clicked" and sadly their projects were abandoned.

You, however, emerged victorious. You've got your game engine of choice, you are comfortable enough with it to implement *The Video Game Building Blocks*, and maybe you've even done a game jam. You are *making the game you want to play*, and you've *found the fun*. This is not easy stuff and you should be proud of your accomplishments thus far.

Now it's time to start thinking about how to wrap up a finished game idea out of these puzzle pieces. Your game, envisioned in its entirety, is its **scope**. Everyone who makes games struggles with scope. Since you're making a game all by yourself it's extra important to keep your scope small and focused.

One way to help with managing scope is by thinking about the **minimum viable product** (MVP). An MVP provides just the bare essentials to get the game concept across (and absolutely nothing else). Using this approach can help you focus on the most important things without getting overwhelmed by all the tasks that inevitably pile up.

Game design pillars are also useful when managing scope. Game design pillars provide direction to a project. If you're making a game about cooking, your game design pillars might include "cooking", "coziness", and "tranquility". When a potential idea comes up for a game, it's useful to refer to the game design pillars to determine whether or not that feature makes sense. For example, a player might suggest that you add bombs to your game ... but does that gel with your game design pillars? I suppose one could cook with a bomb, but does that evoke "coziness" or "tranquility"?

It's important to consider concepts like MVP and game design pillars to help keep your scope in check. Why? Because of one of the most inevitable problems in game development: **scope creep**.

Beware of Scope Creep

Scope creep is a real killer. Scope creep (sometimes called **feature creep**) refers to a project's natural tendency to increase in size over time. Projects can spend months or even years fighting against their own scope. Scope easily expands as new ideas emerge and systems are connected. Scope rarely shrinks on its own.

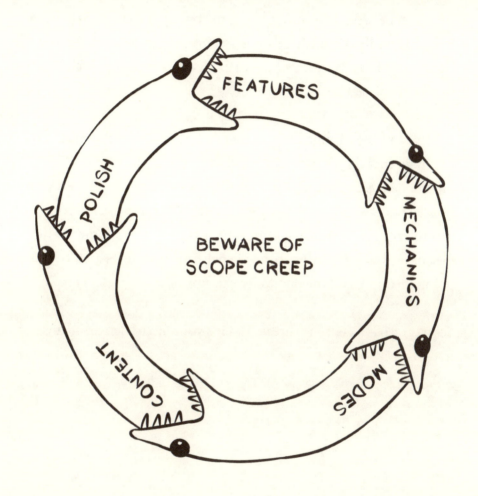

When scope creep gets out of hand, the project's chances of getting finished rapidly diminish. It's a persistent danger. Scope creep is like a multi-headed hydra whose diabolical heads regrow each time they are chopped off.

When climbing Mount Everest, there's a point where the elevation is so high that the air becomes too thin to sustain human life. We human beings cannot survive in this space indefinitely. There's a parallel to draw here with a game's scope. When a project's scope gets too big for its available resources, that project is doomed. The idea of pushing forward becomes exhausting, the lungs aren't doing their job, and the developer can't breathe.

Scope creep is a genuine threat, and it's your job to defend against it.

Remember: You Are a Producer

Hello, producer. What's that on your head?

Oh, you're probably still wearing your beloved hat. Game designer hat, right? Or was it artist, programmer, musician? Whatever the case, take that hat off. Now you are just your pure self, the producer. And the producer cares nothing for your precious hats! Only finishing the game matters.

For this chapter, prepare to make some hard decisions. This is when producing starts to feel like real *work*, because it's painful to be withholding while also trying to make a game that scratches your itch. It's a tough balance and everyone struggles with it.

PERFECTION IS ACHIEVED, NOT WHEN THERE IS NOTHING LEFT TO ADD, BUT WHEN THERE IS NOTHING LEFT TO TAKE AWAY.

ANTOINE DE SAINT EXUPERY

Spoiler: your game will not be perfect. Let go of the idea of perfection and simply allow yourself to create your game, unencumbered, warts and all.

Adhere to the wise words, "Less is more."

PERFECT IS THE
ENEMY OF GOOD.

VOLTAIRE

If perfect is the enemy of good, then scope creep is the enemy of shipping.

A game producer's job is to ship the best game they can as efficiently as they can. Scope creep will be trying to expand in every nook and cranny and it's part of your job to quell that growth.

Moving forward there are no easy answers except, "No."

Cut Deep

I use the word *cut* in this chapter with intent. To finish your game, you're going to have to wield a sharp object and hack away. There will be blood.

I'm serious. Do you have a scalpel? That's not good enough. Get out your machete. You're in the jungle, baby, and the foliage is too thick to push forward. Dense leaves, branches, overgrowth: it's all blocking your path. If the machete isn't doing the job, get out your *chainsaw*!

To know where to cut, think about the core essence of your game. There's probably one singular mechanic that makes it click, that makes it fun. Everything surrounding that one thing should either support it ... or get cut.

While making your game, some really cool pie-in-the-sky ideas will come up that you're excited about. You loved these ideas but you kind of knew in the back of your mind that they were outside of the scope of the project. It's time to say no to those.

It's inevitable that you'll do some work that is outside of scope. Systems and content that you've poured your time and love into will end up being extraneous. Toughen up, because you've got to send them off to the chopping block.

It's hard to kill your darlings. Some of your favorite things could end up being on the cutting room floor. *Chapter 9: Iterate to the Finish Line* provides insight on how to cope with this.

It's totally normal to spend time that feels wasted on areas that end up getting cut. Just remember that the experience of making them was beneficial and (hopefully) fun. In the end, you'll see that the cuts paid off. By cutting things, you made the game better and easier to ship.

KILL YOUR DARLINGS,
KILL YOUR DARLINGS,
EVEN WHEN IT BREAKS YOUR
EGOCENTRIC LITTLE
SCRIBBLER'S HEART,
KILL YOUR DARLINGS.

STEPHEN KING

Must, Should, Could

You should have some method to track what needs to be done in your project. Deep task management is outside the scope of this book, but your solution could be as simple as keeping a list in a `TODO.txt` file in your project's folder, or as complicated as a team-based cross-platform task management application.

These tasks that come up during development could look something like this:

1. Fix crash when player pauses
2. Add a settings menu
3. Get new avatar sprites
4. Implement a critical hit system
5. Improve selection sounds

TYPICAL TODO LIST

1. Fix crash when player pauses
2. Add a settings menu
3. Get new avatar sprites
4. Implement a critical hit system
5. Improve selection sounds

These tasks are often arranged by discipline: artwork, game design, production, programming, sound design, etc. It's also useful to arrange the tasks by importance. Common labels include **Must**, **Should**, and **Could**.

Must refers to a task that is mandatory for a game to ship, **Should** represents a desirable task that is not required, and **Could** means optional. Let's triage our hypothetical tasks using these labels:

Fix crash when player pauses. This is a **Must**. Crashing pretty much always ruins a player's experience and nobody would find that acceptable. The fact that it happens when trying to pause the game (something almost all players will do at some point) means there's a crash along the **critical path**, where all players must exist. This has to be fixed before you can ship.

Add a settings menu. Sounds like a **Should** to me. Most games provide some settings like muting the audio, mapping keyboard keys, or deleting local data. I think it's important but maybe it isn't a high priority for your particular project.

Get new avatar sprites. This depends on the current state of the sprites. If they're all sloppy placeholders, or even sprites "borrowed" from one of your favorite games during development, then this is a **Must**. You can't ship with intellectual property that doesn't belong to you. However (and this is important), if you have serviceable sprites in place but simply don't *love* the current sprites, and would *like* to have new ones ... then this is probably a **Could**.

Implement a critical hit system. This is very likely a **Could** but should be discussed. If your tentative game concept is called *Captain Critical Hit and the Critical Hitters*, then the concept might be incomplete without critical hits, making this a **Must**. If otherwise you've got fun, deep, satisfying gameplay without a critical hit system, then consider closing this task altogether.

Improve selection sounds. Seems like a **Could**. Unless the selection sounds mentioned are offensive to the ears then the game can probably ship without this task completed.

The Must, Should, Could pattern is very common and useful, but it's not a perfect model for whether a task will or will not get done. In your mind's eye, imagine the state of the project 10 years from now. Did the Should or Could tasks get done? From my experience a finished game almost always has a backlog of Should and Could tasks that ended up getting closed after the project shipped. As far as the future is concerned, all that really matters are the Must tasks.

As a producer, you might consider limiting your priorities. Must, Should, and Could are conventional, and a decent place to start. But down the road when the project is finished, all that really matters is what got done and what did not. For that reason, using only Must and Could may help simplify things for you.

Whatever process you decide for tracking your tasks, ensure it gets out of your way and helps push you forward.

"COULD" IS REALLY JUST A DOCUMENT OF YOUR GAME IDEAS.

GEOFF BLAIR

What If You Shipped Tomorrow?

WHOA! You weren't prepared for this, right? It would be impossible to finish your game by tomorrow ... wouldn't it?

It depends on the game of course, but some developers can ship small, impressive games in as little as a weekend. Granted, they usually have years of experience and finely-tuned tools that they know how to use expertly. Obviously I don't actually expect you to finish your game tomorrow, but entertaining the idea is a useful practice for keeping scope under control.

With barely any time left, right away you can remove all tasks that are below the Must label. Should, Could, whatever: none of that is happening. As the producer you're saying a hard NO to everything else and thinking only about how to finish the game.

Think about what truly are Must tasks. Consider the rest out of scope for a moment to see how it impacts your priorities.

Chapter 8: The Player Experience

It's time to start thinking about what players experience when they play your game. What's it like to play your game? Do players know what to do? If they get off track, can they get back on track? Is it configurable enough?

User experience (UX) refers to a person's emotions, perceptions, and responses when they use a product, or in your case, play a game. UX is an entire discipline and industry all its own, with a specific branch dedicated to games. So we can't cover everything, but let's discuss some common UX topics and how you should think about them while making your video game.

First-time user experience: Sometimes called the **new user experience**, this refers to what players go through when they interact with your game for the first time. It is arguably one of the most important aspects of your game, since players who initially have a terrible experience may not want to continue playing. You could tackle the first-time user experience with a few simple text prompts or a complex tutorial system.

Game flow: A game needs good pacing and progression to ease players into the game. Your game will probably have many interesting challenges or puzzles that players must get through, ranging dramatically in difficulty. It's important to give players a steady drip of new challenges instead of dumping everything on them at once.

Player motivation: Your game should feel compelling and rewarding. Players should want to continue playing and should be able to explain why. Are they interested to see the next level because the new environments are so pretty? Do they keep failing but want to give it "one more try" because they're enjoying the challenge? Keep your players entertained, excited, and motivated.

Cognitive load: Don't overwhelm your player. Cognitive load refers to the working memory a player needs to retain in order to understand how to play your game. We've all seen games with dozens of menus, icons, and tiny text, covering the bulk of the screen. These situations can feel overwhelming because the human brain can only comfortably juggle so much at once.

Clarity: The player should always know what their goal is, what state the game is in, and how well they're doing. If these things aren't always obvious, it might be time to clean up your presentation. Make things as clear as possible.

Controls: The way the player provides input to your game should be intuitive and obvious. Players should feel confident and in control. Input should also follow industry and platform conventions. For example, on English computer keyboards the `WASD` keys are conventionally used for orthogonal movement. Many players will have this muscle memory built in, so unless your game has a compelling reason to break convention, you may as well adopt it to ease the onboarding process for them.

User Interface (UI): Your game will likely need buttons, knobs, panels, or icons to communicate with the player. Always ensure that interactive elements look interactive — for example, buttons should look pressable. Again there is convention to consider: red often means negative (like deleting files), and green often means good (like saving files). Maintain consistency between elements.

Feedback: Players don't know what you don't tell them. Let them know when they did well, and let them know when they messed up. If a player beats a difficult challenge, give them a little show: play a happy sound, show an animation, or bounce some congratulatory text. Likewise if a player failed, let them know.

Error prevention and recovery: Players will very likely end up in error states, where they are simply not understanding how to proceed. In some games (like puzzle games) this is half the fun, but sometimes the real problem is that the game should be communicating itself better. Games are so vast in their diversity that it's hard to cover all possibilities, but these error states can often be prevented by highlighting buttons the player needs to press or guiding the player with level design hints.

Solve Problems

Your video game will have problems and it's your job to solve them. A good place to start is with your own problems, so begin by streamlining the experience for yourself.

Spend time playing and enjoying your game, looking out for any areas that are confusing, slow, or aren't as fun as they could be. Is there a clunky interface? Is a given monster annoying to fight? Did you get lost in a badly designed level? Were you unable to find an important setting? Take note of these problems and start to think about how best to solve them.

To emphasize potential pain points, try playing through your game as fast as you can. Which parts are fun and breezy? Which parts are slow and cumbersome? The slow areas are good candidates to investigate for improvement.

Also imagine what problems a brand new player would encounter in your game. You can simulate this experience while playing yourself: play your game, pretending like you have no idea what it's about. Play it in the role of someone confused and stumbling through the experience. Try to forget everything you know about what the game is asking of the player. Try to do the wrong things and break it.

You may be surprised by how many problems you can find (and solve) in this manner.

Watch & Learn

Once you've gleaned all you can from your own experience playing your game, it's time to enlist the help of others. You are making this game by yourself, but as we discussed, nobody works completely alone. Your video game will benefit if you watch others play it and learn from what you see.

A **playtest** is a session where one or more participants play your game while you observe their behavior. Professional playtest setups can be complicated and expensive, but for our purposes, you can just have a friend sit at your computer while you are nearby recording information. Or do a video call and have your participant share their screen.

During playtests, resist the urge to speak. You will be tempted to nudge players in the directions you want them to go, but doing so often prevents you from learning more. Simply sit back, watch the player, and take notes.

WATCH YOUR PLAYERS PLAY
AND KEEP YOUR MOUTH SHUT.

ANDREA ABNEY

If a player asks a question such as, "How do I do X?" or "Where's the Y?" you should resist the urge to answer directly. Instead, try asking them what *they* think is the answer. This gives you insight into what they're thinking and will often surprise you. At a certain point you can nudge players in the direction you want them to go, but only after you're sure you've extracted whatever lessons you can from the situation.

You only really need a handful of playtests before you learn most of what you need to know for the time being. After that, you see the same problems arise and receive diminishing returns on the value of the time spent playtesting. Once you've fixed most issues that came up from the first round of playtests, you can repeat the process as many times as you feel you need to.

To find playtesters, a great place to start is with your friends or family members. I think you'll find that many of them are receptive to the idea and will be happy to volunteer their time to help you. Shy playtesters can sometimes be convinced to help you by getting a playtester credit in the game (that's nice to do for anyone donating their time to your project).

To expand your search and find additional playtesters, put your web search skills to use. You may find friendly fellow game developers who would be happy to play your game and provide feedback. Set up a situation where you can watch them in real time, if possible. There are also websites that will run remote playtests for you. For those that can afford it, the expense can be reasonable and pay dividends on improving your player experience.

Apply Oil

Occasionally you might wander around your home to find creaking doors, oiling them so they no longer make annoying sounds. Or maybe you have a wooden staircase that groans when you walk on it. When living in your home, taking a few minutes to hammer a nail in a certain spot could make all the difference. Suddenly you find yourself no longer avoiding the stairs and enjoying your life more.

Oil can also be applied to various parts of your video game. Independent game developer Lars Doucet (*Defender's Quest*) wrote about the concept of oil as pertains to game design. Simply put: oil makes input easier.

OIL IS ABOUT MINIMIZING THE FRICTION AND EFFORT THAT GOES INTO MAKING AN INPUT.

LARS DOUCET

If your game is doing anything to reduce the fun, that's a squeaky wheel that needs to be oiled. In the original *The Legend of Zelda*, the character Link moves freely around the screen. It feels good to walk around, to navigate the grid. Why does this game feel better than many similar games? It's because the *Zelda* developers smartly oiled one of their core mechanics.

When Link is moving by impassable objects, players benefit from a subtle system that gently nudges Link away from the obstacle, enabling smooth passage. In games where this mechanic is not oiled, the player avatar bumps up against the wall, unable to move forward, just barely caught on the corner. This can create a frustrating player experience, doesn't feel good, and benefits from being oiled.

The player experience is an important consideration in a video game and unfortunately something that's often overlooked. Time spent solving problems and applying oil is well spent as you continue pushing towards the finish line.

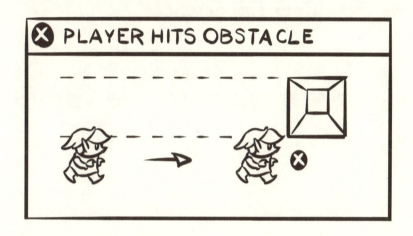

The Developer Experience

Going further, what's it like to develop the game? Is anything particularly painful or slow? Do you find yourself dreading certain parts of the game's creation because the experience is less than ideal?

Don't live with a thorn in your side; take a moment to remove it. The overall goal is to make a video game with a great player experience, but it's also important to recognize your own quality of life as the sole developer.

GREAT TOOLS HELP
MAKE GREAT GAMES.

JOHN ROMERO

For certain pain points, it might be worth taking a little time to develop a small, specialized tool for yourself. Be on the lookout for any task that you find yourself doing over and over, that you could perhaps automate away.

I do lots of 2D sprite work, so I often need to perform menial tasks like arranging cells in a sheet, or separating all sprites by 2 pixels. These tasks are boring and time-consuming for humans but easy and fast for computers. In these cases I'll often take a couple of hours to create a little script for myself that I can call anytime to automate the task for me. This time almost always feels well spent.

Ensure that you feel empowered when creating your game. You should be confident when designing levels, puzzles, or similar content. If it's a struggle, consider easing the pain by using your video game producing skills. Search for tools or make your own.

Don't go off the deep end — if you're making a tool for yourself and start having thoughts like, "Hmm maybe this map editor should be a separate project. I could package it up and sell it on the mar—" STOP! You've gone too far.

Make a tight, concise tool just for you that solves only the problems *you* have, and that's it. Anything else is out of scope.

A GOOD IDEA IS SOMETHING THAT DOES NOT SOLVE JUST ONE SINGLE PROBLEM, BUT RATHER CAN SOLVE MULTIPLE PROBLEMS AT ONCE.

SHIGERU MIYAMOTO

One kind of tool that I like to build for myself for almost every game I work on is a **playground**. A playground is a hidden area in the game, available only to you as the developer. It's a quick entry point you can use to test new content, figure out bugs, and feel at home.

A playground is a good idea because it gives you a quick entry point to test a particular game state, plus it gives you a hidden, secret "home" within your game. It's some space to carve out and call your own. It endears the project to you and helps you continue loving it through good times and bad.

You can quickly jump into your playground to test functionality easily. Throw entities around, experiment with level design — put whatever you want wherever you want. In your playground, messy is fine. This is just for you, kept away from the players. It doesn't need to be tidy, and in fact should be comfortable, lived-in, cozy.

If clean and tidy is your thing, go for it! It's *your* playground and if you want it well organized, that's your business.

This playground should be cut off, isolated, and unable to cause bugs in other parts of the game. Think of your playground as a laboratory where you are a powerful mad scientist, capable of creating or destroying entire worlds. Here you can perform focused experiments to zap bugs, or go wild and throw things together just to see what happens.

Add weird things to your playground that are just for you. This is a reminder that this game is uniquely yours and the playground should especially represent that. In your playground, you're in control.

Your playground can be a workshop where you have just one squeaky door at a time that you are oiling. It allows you to focus on solving one problem without worrying about all the others. The playground is an ideal place to concentrate on improving the player (and developer) experience.

MAKE A PLAYGROUND

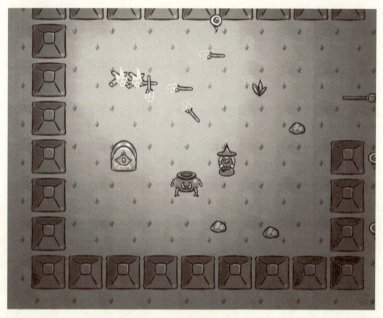

Messy or clean, however you like it.

Chapter 9: Iterate to the Finish Line

Here be dragons, multi-headed hydras, whatever ... the previous bosses were nothing compared to the *final* boss: **Finishing**.

Prior bosses were big, robust, and spongy, but they were at least large enough to be easy targets to hit. This final **swarm boss** is like Dracula in the form of 1,000 bats that you must face individually.

This swarm must be dispatched but there's no silver bullet or magic bomb that'll destroy the whole thing. It's pulling a weed only for two more to sprout up. It's defeating a zombie horde only to find another around the corner. Many projects will succumb to this death by a thousand cuts.

What causes this swarm boss to spawn? Many factors ...

Technical debt (or **code debt**) accrues as any complicated software project is built: the easy path was chosen at some point that now needs to be refactored, or a library is out of date and requires a refresh, or something you've "been meaning to fix" finally becomes mandatory before you can move forward. Some of this debt is inevitable and must be paid eventually.

Source code solidifies over time, like drying cement. As systems increase in complexity they become more tightly coupled, rigid, and difficult to change. Edge cases were fixed, causing intermingled logic exceptions that make the code harder to untangle than it was during earlier stages of the project.

As time rolls by you'll be learning so much that your **personal tastes may change**. Art you made or sourced a while ago no longer appeals to you. Your opinion of how to name files improved and now it all looks "incorrect" to your eyes. Your coding style has upgraded and now you feel the need to do mass find/replace commands or minor refactors. The important thing is to always be pushing towards the finish line and not just spinning your wheels.

IT'S EASY TO GET SO WRAPPED UP IN THE CODE ITSELF THAT YOU LOSE SIGHT OF THE FACT THAT YOU'RE TRYING TO SHIP A GAME.

ROBERT NYSTROM

This final boss has many forms. One of them is like a virus that attacks your immune system. It infects you with sickness and **saps your energy**. Your project is powered by your energy alone, so be extra wary of this kind of attack.

How to defend against this attack: Take breaks when you need to. Play the long game: rest, recover, and return only when ready.

The swarm boss has another form with a **psychological attack**, focused on the mind. This attack can cause you to second-guess yourself, to start asking yourself questions like, "Is this the right project?" or "What's the point of all this?" Your mind will wander and your desire to start fresh new projects may rise.

How to defend against this attack: Not all battles can be won with swords, guns, or fire. To defend against this attack you may need to have an honest debate with yourself and argue for your project. Revisit *Chapter 2: Scratch Your Itch*. Is this project scratching your itch? Is this itch strong enough? It might be time to rest and reflect … or go exploring for inspiration.

> THE FIRST 90% OF THE CODE ACCOUNTS FOR THE FIRST 90% OF THE DEVELOPMENT TIME. THE REMAINING 10% OF THE CODE ACCOUNTS FOR THE OTHER 90% OF THE DEVELOPMENT TIME.
>
> TOM CARGILL

If you feel the urge to explore a different approach or even a new project, consider allowing yourself to do so temporarily. You'll either find that the new project is more acutely scratching your itch or that the grass isn't greener, and return to finishing the previous project. Just don't hop back and forth forever; eventually you need to commit.

Prepare for more. This final swarm boss also has a fourth form. And a fifth. And maybe a sixth, seventh, eighth ...

I DECIDED TO PUT ASIDE
MY MAIN PROJECT AND JUST
WORK ON THIS TINY LITTLE
PROJECT.

ADAM ROBINSON-YU

Complete the Loop

It's time to wrap up those loose ends.

Ensure your game has a beginning, a middle, and an end. Allow players to enter the game, start it up, have some fun, then shut it down. Think of your game as having bookends, providing a sense of finality. A feeling of having started and a feeling of completion.

An **evergreen game** is one that a player can play every day, essentially forever. Some classic evergreen examples include *Sudoku*, *Solitaire*, *Animal Crossing*, and *Triple Town*. Players can (and do) play these games on a daily basis because the games offer them experiences that remain fresh between sessions.

Video games are so vast and complicated that it's sometimes difficult to think about them having beginnings, middles, and ends. But even evergreen games have these traits. Players are human beings and incapable of playing a game forever. Our bodies need breaks for rest, food, sleep, and a variety of stimuli.

Some of these games continue on without the players, with persistent simulated worlds like those found in *World of Warcraft* or *Star Citizen*. But the individual player experience still has a beginning, a middle, and an end.

Whatever loose ends there are, it's time to tie them together. Complete the loop.

Quality of Life

Something that often gets overlooked until the later stages of game development is what's sometimes referred to as a game's **quality of life**. Quality of life includes access to important components like a title screen, credits, settings, preferences, managing game states, and perhaps more depending on your game's functionality.

An **accessible** game is one that can be comfortably played by anyone regardless of varying abilities or access to certain inputs. A game accessibility deep dive is outside the scope of this book, but keep in mind that not everyone experiences colors the same way or can adhere to your input requirements.

Sometimes providing a simple quality of life setting can make the difference between someone enjoying your game or not.

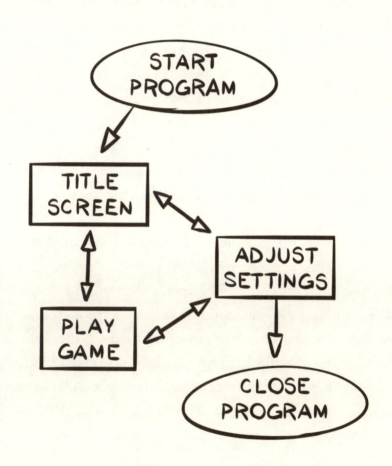

Think about how players will experience your game as a flow chart. They start up the game, probably enter at a title screen, have the ability to adjust settings, can create or enter a game session (perhaps with configuration options), should be able to exit whenever they want, and can repeat these steps without issue.

Human beings need air, water, food, and shelter to survive. Human players need to be able to easily start, configure, end, and resume a video game to have a high quality of life in the game.

For many of us, these quality of life tasks can be a real drain. We all have our itches, whatever is inspiring us to create video games, and this stuff is rarely it. Beautiful graphics, elegant game designs, digital worlds, satisfying sound effects, and gorgeous soundtracks are usually among what drives us to make video games with our precious time. Menus, buttons, scrollbars, data management, and configurable input is far from that … but they're still important. Keep the finish line in sight and find a way to power through all tasks in your way.

GAME DESIGN SEEMS GLAMOROUS AND PRESTIGIOUS BUT THEY NEVER TELL YOU THAT YOU'LL SPEND FOUR HOURS TRYING TO GET A BUTTON TO GET BIGGER WHEN YOU MOUSE OVER IT.

LIZ ENGLAND

Keep It Playable

Sometimes you'll need to refactor a portion of code, redesign a core mechanic, or bulldoze some content. While performing all these major surgeries it's important to keep the game playable from start to finish. That way you've always got something solid to demonstrate, something ready to play, something happy to scratch your itch.

ALWAYS MAINTAIN
CONSTANTLY SHIPPABLE
CODE.

JOHN ROMERO

As you refactor, build safely alongside other features rather than crippling them. Let's say hypothetically you're making a shooter game and decided to revisit your weapon firing mechanic so that the system can support multiple types of projectiles instead of just one. There are a few ways to approach this, including:

1. Rip out the old system entirely, then build a brand new weapon firing system from scratch.
2. Gut the current system, replacing it with a new one while you work (kind of like a parasite taking over a host's body).
3. Build the new system in tandem alongside the preexisting system.

In the past I've executed versions of all three approaches, and let me tell you from experience that you should *build the new system in tandem alongside the preexisting system* whenever that's an option. Here's why:

KEEP OLD SYSTEMS INTACT WHEN BUILDING REPLACEMENT SYSTEMS

 OLD SYSTEM (INTACT & HAPPY)

❌ DON'T GUT OR DESTROY

✓ DO BUILD ALONGSIDE

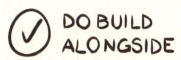

OLD — NEW — OLD — NEW

The previous system remains functional. The game doesn't suffer while the operation happens. If you ever need to step away from the project for a while, it can be frustrating to return to a broken state. It hurts a project's momentum.

The previous system is there as a reference point. The new system will likely have much in common with the old one, making it useful to have the old system intact so that you can reference it while you work on the new one. You can't do that if you're actively crippling the previous system.

Once you're done building the new system alongside the old, you can basically just "flip a switch" to the new system. Working nondestructively in this way is like performing less invasive surgery on a patient. It's healthy and good practice.

There are also many things you should **not** be doing while fighting the swarm boss, including:

- **Don't** add hungry things that come with extra baggage.
- **Don't** add something that breaks stuff (even if you intend to fix it later).
- **Don't** add something that isn't up to the level of polish as everything else.
- **Don't** set traps for your future self!

If you *must* make a change that breaks things, make sure it's temporary and have a plan to revert to a backup if it doesn't go well. **Version control** lets you keep track of granular changes to your project. Version control is trivial to set up and (in my opinion) mandatory for any video game project. I recommend a popular, open source system called *Git* but your options are myriad. The goal is just for it to be easy for you to revert to previous versions of your game at any time.

Games are made to be played. You're going to be doing a lot of invasive surgery on your game but always keep it playable.

There's Always More To Do

Making a video game (especially by yourself) can take what feels like forever. Finishing is one of the hardest parts of game development. At this point you are standing on a pile of the corpses of your peers. You're up to your chest in mud. Pressing forward is slow and taxing.

Sometimes you'll complete a large task only to find another looming right behind it. Sometimes you knew it was coming and other times you'll feel totally blindsided. Another task to throw in the big pile of tasks ...

... and another ...

Get comfortable being in this state. Keep the finish line in sight, but don't kid yourself that it's closer than it is. Time and time again you'll feel like you're almost at the goal, only to realize that you're nowhere near it. Behave as if there are still huge tasks you must complete before you're finished, because there usually are.

Don't pull your game out of the oven too soon. Let it bake. Let it percolate. Play it every day and listen. Ask yourself if it's speaking to you. Is it asking for anything? It might be saying, "Look, you've *really* gotta fix that one bug you've been putting off." Or, "Let's be honest, the first level needs to be redesigned."

Your video game will be in this "I'm just trying to finish it" phase for what feels like too long. It's normal and okay, so long as you actually are being productive and moving towards the finish line.

Be patient, persistent, and push forward. It'll get there.

I NEED TO REMIND MYSELF THAT I SHOULD BE WORKING TOWARDS AN END GOAL AND NOT JUST WORKING. IT'S VERY EASY TO BE BUSY, BUT THAT DOESN'T MEAN THAT YOU'RE PRODUCTIVE.

JAN WILLEM NIJMAN

Save It For the Sequel

You can't work on your game forever; at some point you've got to decide that it's good enough and that you'll finish what you've made. If you're having a hard time deciding when to call it done, refer again to *Chapter 7: Manage Your Scope*. When you've got an MVP that adheres to your game design pillars, you may be ready to wrap it up.

Critical bugs must be fixed. Crashes must be prevented. Data loss must be corrected. But at this stage, almost anything else is at best a Probably Not task. If a feature or piece of content is incomplete, cut it. As the producer, it's now your job to crush those dreams, say no to as much as possible, and focus on finishing.

Here's a way to help ease the pain of saying no to so much: tell yourself you will **save it for the sequel**. This takes the burden off of the project without completely denying or destroying the idea behind the task.

Say you want to add a cool fire sword or a clever puzzle mechanic. Maybe it's exciting to you and saying "no" feels like leaving an itch unscratched. That's okay, because maybe you'll make a sequel some day. Remove the task from your plate and relocate it to your list of sequel tasks. You get to keep the cool idea around but it won't prevent you from finishing your game. Also: maybe the list of sequel tasks will motivate you to finish *this* game so you can eventually spend your time on the sequel. Bonus!

Keep iterating with a focus on finishing the game in front of you. For everything else, save it for the sequel.

Chapter 10: Ship It!

The road has been long and arduous, but you have done it! The dragons are slain, the hydras decapitated, and the swarm depleted. Welcome to the finish line. Take a moment to relax and collect yourself. You've earned it.

At this point, you should have a largely complete video game. You've produced it all by yourself. It scratches your itch, it's the game you want to play, you found the fun, you managed to keep the scope down, you crafted a great player experience, and you iterated to the finish line.

So what's next?

You Have Agency

This book is interactive, which means you have **agency**. Agency is the ability to express yourself and make your own decisions.

There could be an entire guide much larger than this one focused only on how to release your game to the world. How to prepare it, market it, sell it, how to find and make publisher deals, what to charge, which platforms to concentrate on, how to build an audience ... the list goes on and on. This book is not that. You've made a video game and that was our mission.

There are more games being released than ever before. Every day, hundreds or even thousands of new games are released on various platforms across the globe. Perhaps you're ready to send your beloved video game off to fight that war. Or perhaps not yet.

Nobody can tell you where to go from here. Nobody can tell you what to do with your video game, nor when it is finished. It's up to you.

Why Release?

There are many reasons to release your game. For one, releasing can give you a feeling of completion. The ability to move on, to focus on something new, something exciting. The freedom to seek out new ideas and to *save it for the sequel*.

Releasing can also give you a valuable portfolio piece. A released video game can gather precious eyeballs, recognizing your work and putting it in front of people who might be able to make a positive impact on your life. Releasing can give you a boost of confidence, a validation of your work.

Importantly, there are some lessons you can *only* learn by releasing. You'll have surprising experiences that you never expected. You'll be exposed to new bugs. You'll receive thoughtful, piercing insights from players. Releasing gives you perspective that only releasing can give you. You may be excited to release your video game … and maybe you'll do it right away. But remember: *you have agency*.

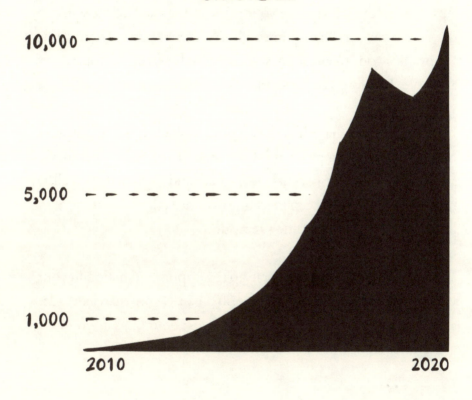

Why Not Release?

Part of releasing is giving up your game to the world. Sure you own the source code and have some rights to certain parts of your game ... but once you *release*, it doesn't completely belong to you anymore. It belongs to the world.

It will get played, that much is certain. It will likely also get stolen, hated, stomped, mangled, and desecrated. If you're lucky, it may also get enjoyed, praised, cheered, shared, and adored. This is all normal and fine. Just keep in mind that once released, you have little control over your game's reception.

You may also be signing yourself up to support and maintain your video game for much longer than you'd like. (More than a decade after release, I still sometimes get messages about bugs in my old games that I'd now rather not worry about.)

> FORTUNE FAVORS
> THE PREPARED MIND.
>
> LOUIS PASTEUR

A finished but unreleased video game can be a valuable tool for tapping into unexpected opportunities. Perhaps you live with your game for a while, deciding what to do with it, and you come upon a licensing deal. For several years, my independent game company *Lost Decade Games* survived mostly on white-label licensing deals which involved branding our games for other platforms. Some of these deals called for an **exclusive license**, which is a unique license to distribute a game, and can only be sold once. Releasing elsewhere means being unable to sell such a license. This will be irrelevant to many of you who do not care about making money with your games, but it's good to be aware of what's out there. Other opportunities may arise that are similar but more relevant to you and your game.

Maybe before releasing you want to gather players. Many developers provide access to what they call a **private alpha** or a **closed beta** — essentially these are versions of the game where it's understood that it's playable, but not finished. This half-step gives the developer an opportunity to get players interested in a game without yet fully committing to calling it done.

Let It Bake

Just wait a moment. Take a breath.

There's so much immediacy in life, especially in the games industry. There's a constant demand for *more* and *now* ...

Take a step away from the mad vortex and constant churn of new content. A video game takes a long time to make. So much time put into a single project can create intense feelings around it. Be patient with yourself and your decisions.

You made a video game, not *for* the world, but *for you*. Spend time with it, get to know it. Wait until it's truly ready in your eyes, complete and concise, with something to say, spoken in your voice.

Some of you are reading this book because you admire developers who made video games "all by themselves" (with help from others, of course). For many of these stories, it took that developer *years* to finish. Let's look at some classics and their development times:

- *Undertale* by Toby Fox: almost **3 years**
- *Braid* by Jonathan Blow: about **3 years**
- *Dust: An Elysian Tail* by Dean Dodrill: over **3 years**
- *Stardew Valley* by Eric Barone: **4.5 years**
- *Axiom Verge* by Tom Happ: **5 years**
- *Cave Story* by Daisuke Amaya: **5 years**

Any of these games could have been released early or incomplete. Instead, they were allowed the proper time to bake in the oven, allowed to cook for however long was needed. Think of your video game as a burger, ready to eat. Imagine a bun and a burger patty of your choice. Simple and delicious. Over time, you could add additional layers. Add cheese, vegetables, or your favorite sauce. It can improve slowly, always ready to eat but not served until you decide it's time.

FINISH, IMPROVE

"FINISHED"   MORE LOVE   EVEN MORE!

If you're working on your *very first* video game, I urge you to finish something short and simple before dedicating many months or (gasp) years to one huge project. Learn the tech, design a *tiny* game that you love, prototype it, and ship it. Making video games is extremely complicated but sometimes creativity is as simple as making things and putting them out there.

You don't need to make your magnum opus, your one true masterpiece (at least, not yet). I know that some of you reading this have grand ambitions, visions of an epic universe that *only you* can create. I want you to succeed because I want to play those amazing games, but it takes time and practice to execute grand ambitions. Make small games to build up your skills before increasing scope.

Just as it's risky to run a marathon without training, it's risky to embark on a long-term video game project without practice and experience.

I know some of you will ignore this warning, and I wish you luck. Just be careful: great risk doesn't always come with great reward.

YOU WILL BE FIERCE.
YOU WILL BE A WARRIOR.
AND YOU WILL MAKE THINGS
THAT AREN'T AS GOOD AS
YOU KNOW IN YOUR HEART
YOU WANT THEM TO BE.
AND YOU'LL JUST MAKE
ONE AFTER ANOTHER.

IRA GLASS

The Video Game Release Checklist

You have agency, and the choice is yours. You've read the pros and cons of whether to release or not and perhaps you've decided it's time to release. It might be scary but it's going to feel good getting it out into the world.

Self-publishing can be as easy as uploading your game files to a web server somewhere and telling a friend. Maybe that's all that you really care about. That's fine.

For many of you, I'm sure that having a sort of "real" release is part of the itch that you want to scratch. You want to put something out there that feels at least semi-professional, something that looks and feels legitimate, something of which you can be genuinely proud. For you, here's what needs to be done to have a "proper" video game release:

1. Get your build ready
2. Write about your game
3. Prepare key assets
4. Gather screenshots and video
5. Create a short trailer
6. Create a press kit
7. Prepare on target platforms
8. Push the button
9. Tell everyone

As the producer, these tasks are in your way. Let's talk about how to get them done.

Get your build ready. You'll need a playable build of your game, ready for distribution. Depending on your unique project that could be a downloadable `.exe` file, availability on a mobile app store, a physical print, or simply a web URL. However your game gets into players' hands, that needs to be prepared and ready to go.

Write about your game. Even if it's out of your comfort zone, you'll need to write a little something about your game. You should have a snappy, single-sentence **elevator pitch**, which is a short, enticing description of your game that any stranger should be able to easily understand (and maybe even find interesting).

Additionally, some platforms require longer descriptions ranging from a few hundred words to sometimes over 1,000 words. Check your target platforms and get all that done.

Prepare key assets. It's helpful (and on some platforms, mandatory) to have images handy that represent your game. An **icon** is a simple, square image that brings your game to mind at a quick glance. They should be uncomplicated in design because they can range dramatically in size from as small as 16x16 pixels to over ten times larger.

Key art is a large, typically more detailed image that represents your game. It's intended to be shown on a cover, as a header at the top of a web page, or even on a poster. **Banners** range wildly in aspect ratio, sometimes needing to be tall and skinny and other times needing to be short and wide. Banners are often based on the key art.

Some producers make their own key art but you could also commission an artist to help you. When in doubt, it's hard to go wrong with imagery directly from your actual video game.

PIXEL WASHER
PROMOTIONAL IMAGES

WIDE BANNER

16x16 ICON

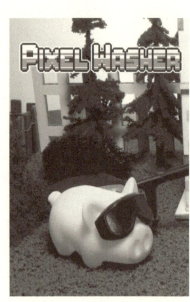

TALL BANNER

Gather screenshots and video. As someone skilled enough with technology to create a video game by yourself, *how* to gather screenshots should be no challenge to you. *Which* screenshots to use is harder. When taking screenshots, get as many as you can, then sort through the good ones: focus on screenshots where the action is clear, it's easily understandable, and it's as exciting as possible. Show your game's diversity. Look for high contrast images with dramatic shifts in light or color.

Create a short trailer. All you need for this step is a short video that quickly presents the name of your game, shows what it's about, and informs the viewer where (and when) to get the game. Be careful here, because it's easy to get lost in the weeds. Video is complicated, editing software can be cumbersome and expensive, and there are a million ways to make a trailer. Just *don't overthink it*, and either bang out something quick and exciting yourself, or find someone to help you.

The best video game trailers feature mostly gameplay and last only 60 seconds or less. Be terse. Catchy music is good, lots of text is usually not.

Create a press kit. A **press kit** (also called a **media kit**) is a web page or downloadable `.zip` file that contains information about a video game. It's useful to authors who want to create content about your game and players who want to learn more. The structure is relatively loose but usually there's a `.pdf` file with descriptions and images, a collection of screenshots, promotional material, and sometimes brief bios about the developer(s) who made the game.

Prepare on target platforms. Online video game platforms have many requirements and sometimes make you jump through unexpected hoops or make you wait between certain steps. It's time to start filling out all the forms and checking all the boxes. Do everything that is necessary to release except for actually releasing.

Even if you're releasing your video game all by yourself on your own web servers, you'll need to do some preparation. Maybe you've got to make yourself a little splash page, or upload your builds and ensure they can be downloaded. Whatever your process, position your game right at the finish line.

Push the button. At this point, your game should be sitting directly *on* the finish line. You've gone through the checklist, double-checked everything, and you feel completely prepared. Time to push the "release" button everywhere that you need to.

Tell everyone (including me!). Congratulations. You went through all the effort of making a video game all by yourself, followed up with the daunting task of releasing it unto the world. That's huge. You should be proud of that and shout it from the rooftops.

Some of you (including me!) may be a little shy and uncomfortable with self-promotion of any kind. Give yourself a break in this case. People love video games, they love "lone wolf" development stories, and hopefully you've got a unique game that only you could have made. Be generous and allow yourself this one thing.

Be a noisy bird. Sing your song. Tell everyone.

You did it. It wasn't easy, but you got it done.

You are a video game producer!

I'm proud of you.

The End

Your path is your own now. As seasoned game developers will tell you, there is no "correct" way to make a video game. Having done it even once is a huge achievement.

Don't stop here. You've learned so much it would be a shame not to put those skills to use. Continue making video games and flexing those hard-earned muscles.

Remember to be yourself. AAA video games are known to trend towards samey ideas, familiar roads, and common patterns. In order to pay for their expensive development, they're designed to appeal to the masses, which often dilutes their visions. Being able to make a video game all by yourself gives you the opportunity to create a novel experience with a focused concept. Use that to your advantage.

Speak with your unique voice.

WHAT WE WANT EVERYBODY TO DO IS TO FIND THEIR STYLE, THEIR EXPRESSION IN THE MEDIUM. EVERYBODY IS THEIR OWN INDEPENDENT ARTIST AND THEY HAVE SOMETHING VALUABLE TO ADD.

JONATHAN BLOW

Recommended Reading

1. *Spelunky* by Derek Yu
2. *The Art of Game Design* by Jesse Schell
3. *A Theory of Fun for Game Design* by Raph Koster
4. *Masters of Doom* by David Kushner
5. *The First 20 Hours* by Josh Kaufman
6. *The GameDev Business Handbook* by Michael Futter
7. *Creativity, Inc.* by Ed Catmull and Amy Wallace
8. *Steal Like an Artist* by Austin Kleon
9. *100 Demon Dialogues* by Lucy Bellwood
10. *Man's Search for Meaning* by Viktor E. Frankl

For a deep dive on game usability, see also a wonderful book to which my wife Andrea Abney contributed: *Game Usability: Advice from the Experts for Advancing UX Strategy and Practice in Videogames (2nd Edition)*.

Recommended ~~Playing~~ Studying

1. *Joust*
2. *Tetris*
3. *Chess*
4. *QWOP*
5. *Spelunky*
6. *Pipe Dream*
7. *Minesweeper*
8. *Super Metroid*
9. *Into the Breach*
10. *Plants VS Zombies*

By now you can tell I love *Spelunky*. To me it's one of the great indie game stories: humble "all by yourself" origins catapulted to a platinum-selling series. The combination of roguelike and side-scrolling platformer was like discovering peanut butter and jelly. Delicious new combos are out there, and *you* can find them!

What's Next?

1. Disconnect (go for a walk, meditate, or take a shower).
2. Remember that you're a producer (remove all of your hats).
3. Search for your itch (and start to scratch it).
4. Play a bunch of video games (old classics and brand new ones).
5. Explore (play with game engines, draw something, make stuff).

Then give a copy of this book to a friend and discuss! Fuel each other's fires.

References

Finishing a Game by Derek Yu. https://makegames.tumblr.com/post/1136623767/finishing-a-game

The Early Days of id Software by John Romero. https://www.youtube.com/watch?v=E2MIpi8pIvY

Cosmos by Carl Sagan.

On Imposter Syndrome by Tommy Refenes. https://web.archive.org/web/20160319090448/https://tommyrefenes.tumblr.com/post/141157110167/impostor-syndrome

1997 WWDC with Steve Jobs. https://medium.com/@donhopkins/focusing-is-about-saying-no-steve-jobs-wwdc-97-ff0174c171d0

Undertale by Toby Fox. https://undertale.com/

Juice it or lose it by Martin Jonasson & Petri Purho.
https://www.youtube.com/watch?v=Fy0aCDmgnxg

Airman's Odyssey by Antoine de Saint-Exupéry.

On Writing: A Memoir of the Craft by Stephen King.

Oil it or Spoil it! by Lars Doucet.
https://www.fortressofdoors.com/oil-it-or-spoil-it/

Interview with Shigeru Miyamoto.
https://www.eurogamer.net/articles/shigeru-miyamoto-interview

Ninety-ninety rule by Tom Cargill.
https://en.wikipedia.org/wiki/Ninety-ninety_rule

Game Programming Patterns by Robert Nystrom.
https://gameprogrammingpatterns.com/

Crafting A Tiny Open World by Adam Robinson-Yu.
https://www.youtube.com/watch?v=ZW8gWgpptI8&t=185s

Tweet by Liz England.
https://twitter.com/lizardengland/status/1336153766698094592

Eggplant: The Secret Lives of Games Episode 38 with Jan Willem Nijman.
https://twitter.com/eggplantshow/status/1218330758420414464

Number of games released on Steam worldwide from 2004 to 2021.
https://www.statista.com/statistics/552623/number-games-released-steam/

Ira Glass on Storytelling from *This American Life*.
https://www.thisamericanlife.org/extras/ira-glass-on-storytelling

Design Discussion with Casey Muratori and Jonathan Blow.
https://www.youtube.com/watch?v=rowyZyVrFHI&t=6097s

BONUS CONTENT!

UNFINISHED DOODLE

Thank You

This book could only be made thanks to these fine people:

Andrea Abney for being my partner, my little buddy, my everything.

William F. Hackett & Mary L. Hackett for giving me life and the tools to thrive.

Geoff Blair for being my friend and sounding board.

Jim MacDonald for introducing me to video game development.

Jonathan Hackett for valuable feedback and brotherly love.

The Jacksons for being inspirational and supportive.

You, dear reader, for your interest and support.

Thank you for ~~playing~~ reading.

YOUR GAME IDEAS

Continue your game making journey at
VALADRIA.COM

Made in United States
Troutdale, OR
12/08/2024